Y0-DWM-844

Janet at School

Paul White

Photographs by Jeremy Finlay

A John Day Book

Thomas Y. Crowell Company · New York

Other books of the same kind

Don't Forget Tom, Hanne Larsen
Claire and Emma, Diana Peter
Sally Can't See, Palle Petersen

Printed in Great Britain

Library of Congress Cataloging in Publication Data

White, Paul.
  Janet at School.

  "A John Day Book."
1. Physically handicapped children—
Education—Juvenile literature. I. Finlay,
Jeremy. II. Title.
LC 4019.2.W45   371.9'1   77-26681
ISBN 0-381-99556-9
ISBN 0-381-99557-7 lib. bdg.

First Edition
10 9 8 7 6 5 4 3 2 1

Janet's just arrived at school, and she's hanging up her coat. She needs the wheelchair because she can't use her legs.

She moves the chair around the classroom herself, pushing on the wheels. To change direction, she pushes just one wheel.

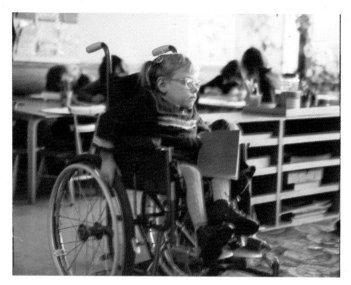

The wheelchair has handles too, so that Janet's friends can push the chair about.

Janet has lots of friends, and in the playground she joins in most of their games. She can't jump rope herself, but she likes turning the rope while the others jump.

Ever since Janet was born, she's been unable to use her legs. That's because there's something wrong with her back—it's called *spina bifida.*

Try feeling down your back. Right down the middle, you can feel a line of bones under the skin. That is your spine. It's the part of your skeleton which holds you up straight when you stand or sit. Without a spine you would flop like jelly.

The spine has another job too. Through the middle of the spine there is a kind of "telephone wire" called the *spinal cord.* The spinal cord takes messages from your brain to your legs and feet.

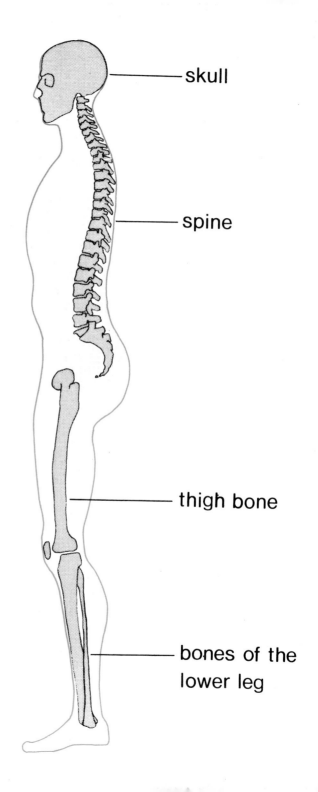

skull

spine

thigh bone

bones of the lower leg

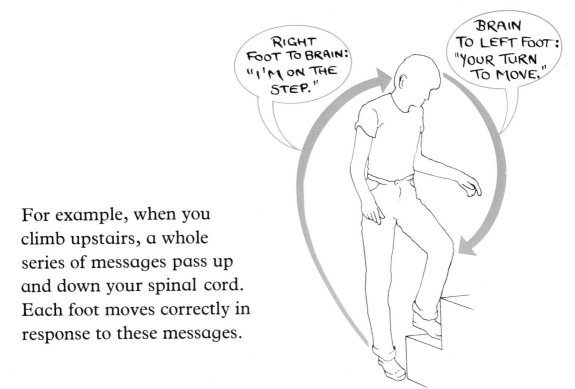

For example, when you climb upstairs, a whole series of messages pass up and down your spinal cord. Each foot moves correctly in response to these messages.

In Janet's spine the spinal cord was damaged even before she was born. Janet has never been able to move her legs because her brain can't send messages to them. Her legs flop down, and she has no feeling in them. She doesn't notice whether they are hot or cold, or even if she gets a cut or bruise.

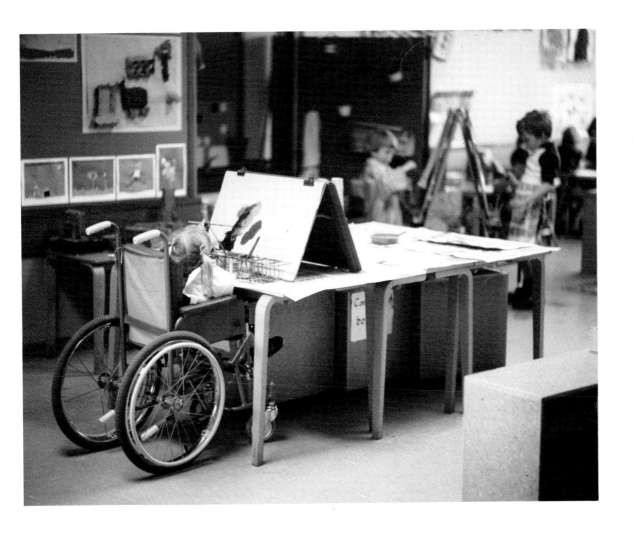

Janet has spent a lot of time in the hospital, but now
she only has to go there four times a year.

Janet doesn't want to sit in her wheelchair all the time, She can sit on the floor and shuffle around on her bottom or lie on her tummy and pull herself along with her arms.

Every day, at school or at home, Janet
does exercises to make her back and arms
stronger.

She can also stand, using metal braces on her legs, but she has to hold on to something or she might topple over.

At the moment everyone is very excited because she is learning to walk, using the braces and this walking frame. Janet is delighted that she will soon be able to walk, but she gets tired quickly.

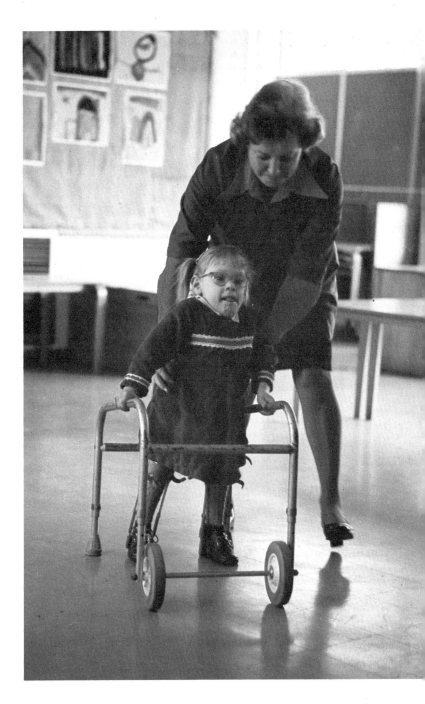

Some things are much harder for Janet than they are for other people. She finds it difficult to stretch out for things, especially if they are high up or just out of reach.

It isn't always easy to bring the wheelchair close enough to a table or sink; Janet also needs help when she goes to the toilet.

When Janet's class is using the equipment in the
school gym, she is as eager as all the others. She can
pull herself up and down these slopes without any
help—which isn't easy just using your arms.

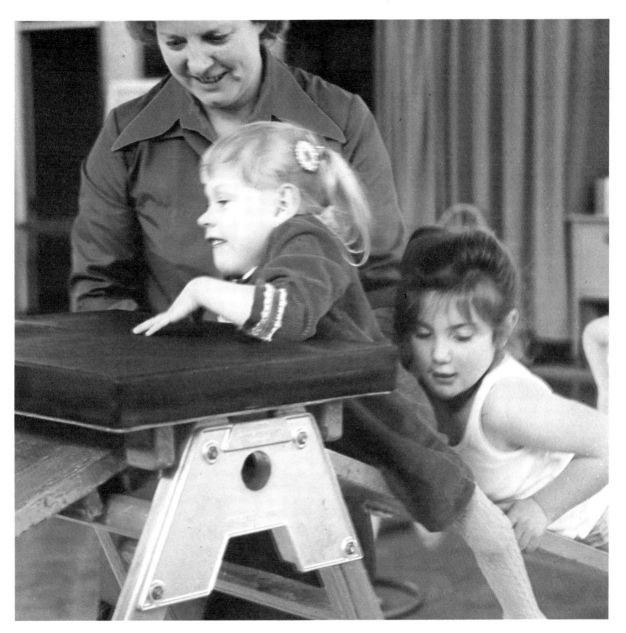

Janet knows that some older people with *spina bifida* have learned to swim, ride a horse, and do sports like archery. She wants to try badminton.

Janet lives just around the corner from
the school, so she can go home to lunch.
Her dad and her big brother Derek come
home too, so lunch is a real family meal.

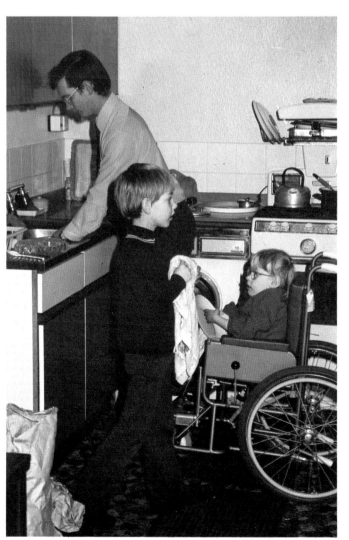

There's usually also time for Janet and Derek to give the rabbit an extra meal, as well as to wash the dishes.

Janet's younger sister, Wendy, can be a bit of a handful. She sometimes spoils Janet's game, and Janet can't move fast enough to stop her.

Janet likes to try things out for herself. She enjoys playing the piano, though she hasn't yet been taught to play it properly.

In the summer the family likes to go camping. They have to find a flat field, because Janet can't move her wheelchair up or down slopes, and she hates having to wait for someone to push her.

The best thing about camping, Derek and Janet agree, is that it is so easy to make new friends. Within minutes of setting up the tent, Derek has friends at the far end of the site, and people come around to Janet's tent. It's not easy for Janet to go to them, so they come to talk and play with her.

If you meet Janet, you may want to know how her
wheelchair works. If so, just ask. She'll probably be
very pleased to show you.